D1109452

...Printing
...er 50,000 in Print
...d's Little Instruction Book for Mom — Special Gift Edition
...BN 1-56292-118-5
...opyright © 1995 by Honor Books, Inc.
P.O. Box 55388
Tulsa, Oklahoma 74155

God's Instruction Book for Mom

INTRODUCTION

God's Little Instruction Book for Mom is an inspirational collection of quotes and Scriptures that will motivate you to live a meaningful, productive and happy life, while meeting and enjoying the challenge and love of being a mom.

Some books have quotes and some have Scripture, but we have combined both to provide not just man's insight, but also the wisdom of God into one of life's most challenging jobs — being a mom. This little book will give you cause to ponder motherhood, but it will also make you laugh. Some of the quotes are well-known and some are obscure, yet each quote includes a Scripture that reveals what God's Word has to say about that topic.

You will find in the last section of the book a collection of humorous and witty quotes that will lighten your load and give you a dose of the "best medicine" — laughter!

This delightful book is basic, practical and filled with the timeless wisdom of the Bible, covering topics that mothers around the world can relate to. *God's Little Instruction Book for Mom* is a welcome break from the fast-paced frenzy of everyday living. We hope that you enjoy and treasure this book as much as we do.

+>———·———<+

*M*others are like fine collectibles — as the years go by they increase in value.

. . . despise not thy mother when she is old.
Proverbs 23:22

Train your child in the way in which you know you should have gone yourself.

C.H. Spurgeon

I will instruct thee and teach thee in the way which thou shalt go: I will guide thee with mine eye.

Psalm 32:8

*A*s a mother, my job is to take care of the possible and trust God with the impossible.

Ruth Bell Graham

And they that know thy name will put their trust in thee: for thou, Lord, hast not forsaken them that seek thee.

Psalm 9:10

When Mother Theresa received her Nobel Prize, she was asked, "What can we do to promote world peace?" She replied, "Go home and love your family."

Let love and faithfulness never leave you; bind them around your neck, write them on the tablet of your heart.

Proverbs 3:3 NIV

You built no great cathedrals
That centuries applaud,
But with a grace exquisite
Your life cathedraled God.

Thomas Fessenden

*...for ye are the temple of the living God; as God hath said,
I will dwell in them, and walk in them....*

2 Corinthians 6:16

Where parents do too much for their children, the children will not do much for themselves.

Elbert Hubbard

The soul of the sluggard desireth, and hath nothing: but the soul of the diligent shall be made fat.

Proverbs 13:4

*I*f we as parents are too busy to listen to our children, how then can they understand a God who hears?

V. Gilbert Beers

Let the wise listen....

Proverbs 1:5 NIV

*N*ever, never be too proud to say, "I'm sorry," to your child when you've made a mistake.

Confess your faults one to another, and pray one for another. . . .

James 5:16

There's a time when you have to explain to your children why they're born, and it's a marvelous thing if you know the reason.

Hazel Scot

Before I (God) formed thee in the belly I knew thee; and before thou camest forth out of the womb I sanctified thee, and I ordained thee....

Jeremiah 1:5

*I*f a child lives with approval, he learns to live with himself.

Dorothy Law Nolte

Wherefore, accept one another just as Christ also accepted us to the glory of God.

Romans 15:7 NAS

The highest pinnacle of the spiritual life is not joy in unbroken sunshine but absolute and undoubting trust in the love of God.

A.W. Thorold

For whatsoever is born of God overcometh the world: and this is the victory that overcometh the world, even our faith.

1 John 5:4

A mother has, perhaps, the
hardest earthly lot; and yet
no mother worthy of the name
ever gave herself thoroughly for her
child who did not feel that, after all,
she reaped what she had sown.

Henry Ward Beecher

And let us not be weary in well doing:
for in due season we shall reap, if we faint not.

Galatians 6:9

Simply having children does not make mothers.

John A. Shedd

...teach the young women to be sober...to love their children.

Titus 2:4

A mother once asked a clergyman when she should begin the education of her child,... "Madam," was the reply,... "From the very first smile that gleams over an infant's cheek, your opportunity begins."

Whately

Train up a child in the way he should go,
even when he is old he will not depart from it.

Proverbs 22:6 NAS

Loving a child is a circular business...the more you give, the more you get, the more you get, the more you give.

Penelope Leach

Give, and it will be given to you.... For by your standard of measure it will be measured to you in return.

Luke 6:38 NAS

*I*f you want your child
to accept your values when
he reaches his teen years,
then you must be worthy
of his respect during
his younger days.

James Dobson

*...in order to offer ourselves as a model for you,
that you might follow our example.*
2 Thessalonians 3:9 NAS

Women should not have children after 35 — 35 children are enough.

Unknown

Happy is the man that hath his quiver full of them....

Psalm 127:5

When we set an example of honesty our children will be honest. When we encircle them with love they will be loving. When we practice tolerance they will be tolerant. When we meet life with laughter and a twinkle in our eye they will develop a sense of humor.

Wilferd A. Peterson

...be thou an example of the believers, in word, in conversation, in charity, in spirit, in faith, in purity.

1 Timothy 4:12

A happy childhood is one of the best gifts that parents have in their power to bestow.

Mary Cholmondeley

Withhold not good from them to whom it is due, when it is in the power of thine hand to do it.

Proverbs 3:27

The family tree is worth bragging about if it has consistently produced good timber, and not just nuts.

Glen Wheeler

A good name is rather to be chosen than great riches....

Proverbs 22:1

There is only one pretty child in the world, and every mother has it.

English Proverb

He hath made every thing beautiful in his time....
Ecclesiastes 3:11

The mother's love is like God's love; He loves us not because we are loveable, but because it is His nature to love, and because we are His children.

Earl Riney

Herein is love, not that we loved God, but that he loved us, and sent his Son to be the propitation for our sins. Beloved, if God so loved us, we ought also to love one another.

1 John 4:10,11

Children spell "love"... T-I-M-E.

Dr. Anthony P. Witham

Don't be fools; be wise: make the most of every opportunity you have for doing good.

Ephesians 5:16 TLB

*I*n practicing the art
of parenthood an ounce
of example is worth a
ton of preachment.

Wilferd A. Peterson

Let your light so shine before men, that they may see your good works, and glorify your Father which is in heaven.

Matthew 5:16

Children are God's apostles, day by day sent forth to preach of love and hope and peace.

Lowell

Behold, children are a gift of the Lord.
Psalm 127:3a NAS

*I*f it is desirable that children be kind, appreciative, and pleasant, those qualities should be taught — not hoped for.

James Dobson

For the commandment is a lamp; and the law is light; and reproofs of instruction are the way of life.

Proverbs 6:23

$\mathcal{A}$ child is fed with milk and praise.

Mary Lamb

Let no corrupt communication proceed out of your mouth, but that which is good to the use of edifying, that it may minister grace unto the hearers.

Ephesians 4:29

A mother is neither cocky, nor proud, because she knows the school principal may call at any minute to report that her child has just driven a motorcycle through the gymnasium.

Mary Kay Blakely

Boast not thyself of tomorrow; for thou knowest not what a day may bring forth.

Proverbs 27:1

*H*ome is the place where the great are small and the small are great.

Glen Wheeler

But many that are first shall be last; and the last shall be first.

Matthew 19:30

You are never so high as when you are on your knees.

Jean Hodges

*Humble yourselves in the sight of the Lord,
and he shall lift you up.*

James 4:10

When home is ruled
according to God's Word,
angels might be asked to
stay with us, and they
would not find themselves
out of their element.

Charles H. Spurgeon

I will meditate in thy precepts, and have respect unto thy ways.
I will delight myself in thy statutes: I will not forget thy word.
Psalm 119:15,16

The best things you can
give children, next
to good habits,
are good memories.

Sydney J. Harris

The memory of the just is blessed....
Proverbs 10:7

Through the ages no nation has had a better friend than the mother who taught her child to pray.

Glen Wheeler

Devote yourselves to prayer, keeping alert in it with an attitude of thanksgiving.

Colossians 4:2 NAS

Give your troubles to God; He will be up all night anyway.

Unknown

He will not allow your foot to slip;
He who keeps you will not slumber.

Psalm 121:3 NAS

We should seize every opportunity to give encouragement. Encouragement is oxygen to the soul.

George M. Adams

A man hath joy by the answer of his mouth:
and a word spoken in due season, how good it is!

Proverbs 15:23

You know children are growing up when they start asking questions that have answers.

John J. Plomb

When I was a child, I spake as a child,
I understood as a child, I thought as a child: but
when I became a man, I put away childish things.

1 Corinthians 13:11

*I*f you want a baby, have a new one. Don't baby the old one.

Jessamyn West

Chasten thy son while there is hope, and let not thy soul spare for his crying.

Proverbs 19:18

*N*ever despair of a child. The one you weep the most for at the mercy-seat may fill your heart with the sweetest joys.

T.L. Cuyler

He that goeth forth and weepeth bearing precious seed, shall doubtless come again with rejoicing. . . .

Psalm 126:6

All that I am or hope to be, I owe to my mother.

Abraham Lincoln

Get all the advice you can and be wise the rest of your life.

Proverbs 19:20 TLB

The best academy, a mother's knee.

James Russell Lowell

Discipline your son, and he will give you peace;
he will bring delight to your soul.

Proverbs 29:17 NIV

Mother means selfless devotion, limitless sacrifice, and love that passes understanding.

Unknown

Greater love hath no man than this,
that a man lay down his life for his friends.

John 15:13

You may give without loving, but you cannot love without giving.

Glen Wheeler

For God so loved the world, that he gave his only begotten Son, that whosoever believeth in him should not perish, but have everlasting life.

John 3:16

A mother is a person who sees that there are only four pieces of pie for five persons and promptly remarks that she's never cared for pie.

Unknown

...It is more blessed to give than to receive.

Acts 20:35

What is a home without a Bible? 'Tis a home where daily bread for the body is provided, but the soul is never fed.'

Charles Meigs

My son, attend to my words; incline thine ear unto my sayings. Let them not depart from thine eyes; keep them in the midst of thine heart. For they are life unto those that find them, and health to all their flesh.

Proverbs 4:20-22

A torn jacket is soon mended; but hard words bruise the heart of a child.

Henry Wadsworth Longfellow

...in accordance with the authority which the Lord gave me, for building up and not for tearing down.

2 Corinthians 13:10 NAS

A mother is not a person to lean on, but a person to make leaning unnecessary.

Dorothy Canfield Fisher

Therefore shall a man leave his father and his mother, and shall cleave unto his wife: and they shall be one flesh.

Genesis 2:24

Of all the rights of women, the greatest is to be a mother.

Lin Yutang

*Her children arise up, and call her blessed;
her husband also, and he praiseth her.*

Proverbs 31:28

Children miss nothing in sizing up their parents. If you are only half convinced of your beliefs, they will quickly discern that fact.

James Dobson

Let us hold fast the profession of our faith without wavering....
Hebrews 10:23

An infallible way to make your child miserable is to satisfy all his demands.

Henry Home

The rod and reproof give wisdom: but a child left to himself bringeth his mother to shame.
Proverbs 29:15

$\mathcal{D}$ear Mother — You know that nothing can ever change what we have always been and will always be to each other.

Franklin Roosevelt

Her children stand and bless her. . . .
Proverbs 31:28

Babies are such a nice way to start people.

Don Herold

...and she conceived...and said,
I have gotten a man from the Lord.

Genesis 4:1

When I come to the end of my rope, God is there to take over.

...for he hath said, I will never leave thee, nor forsake thee.

Hebrews 13:5

A mother understands what a child does not say.

Jewish Proverb

*...serve him with a perfect heart and with a willing mind:
for the Lord searcheth all hearts, and understandeth
all the imaginations of the thoughts....*

1 Chronicles 28:9

Children are natural
mimics — they act like
their parents in spite of
every attempt to teach
them good manners.

Anonymous

Beloved, follow not that which is evil, but that which is good.
3 John 11a

The Lord can do great things through those who don't care who gets the credit.

Helen Pearson

A man's pride shall bring him low: but honour shall uphold the humble in spirit.

Proverbs 29:23

A little boy's mother
once told him that it is
God who makes people good.
He looked up and replied,
"Yes I know it is God,
but mothers help a lot."

Glen Wheeler

. . . reject not nor forsake the teaching of your mother.
Proverbs 1:8

What sunshine is to flowers, smiles are to humanity. They are but trifles, to be sure, but scattered along life's pathway, the good they do is inconceivable.

Joseph Addison

A happy heart makes the face cheerful....
Proverbs 15:13 NIV

I regret often that I have spoken; never that I have been silent.

Syrus

In the multitude of words there wanteth not sin: but he that refraineth his lips is wise.

Proverbs 10:19

Children are likely to live up to what you believe of them.

Lady Bird Johnson

For as he thinketh in his heart, so is he....
Proverbs 23:7

Children are the hands by which we take hold of heaven.

Henry Ward Beecher

Verily I say unto you, Whosoever shall not receive the kingdom of God as a little child shall in no wise enter therein.

Luke 18:17

The persons hardest to convince they're at the retirement age are children at bedtime.

Shannon Fife

Correct thy son, and he shall give thee rest; yea, he shall give delight unto thy soul.

Proverbs 29:17

*M*any parents are finding out that a pat on the back helps develop character — if given often enough, early enough, and low enough.

Glen Wheeler

He that spareth his rod hateth his son: but he that loveth him chasteneth him betimes.

Proverbs 13:24

"*I* can forgive, but I cannot forget,"
is only another way of saying,
"I will not forgive." Forgiveness
ought to be like a canceled note —
torn in two, and burned up, so that
it never can be shown against one.

Henry Ward Beecher

And be ye kind one to another, tenderhearted, forgiving one another, even as God for Christ's sake hath forgiven you.

Ephesians 4:32

Being a full time mother
is one of the highest
salaried jobs in my field
since the payment
is pure love.

Mildred B. Vermont

...for whatsoever a man soweth, that shall he also reap.

Galatians 6:7

*M*otherhood is a partnership with God.

Unknown

For this child I prayed; and the Lord hath given me my petition which I asked of him. Therefore also I have lent him to the Lord; as long as he liveth he shall be lent to the Lord....

1 Samuel 1:27,28

Children need love, especially when they do not deserve it.

Harold S. Hulbert

Be ye therefore merciful, as your Father also is merciful.

Luke 6:36

Too much love never spoils children. Children become spoiled when we substitute "presents" for "presence."

Dr. Anthony P. Witham

We loved you so much that we were delighted to share with you not only the gospel of God but our lives as well, because you had become so dear to us.

1 Thessalonians 2:8 NIV

A man's work is from sun to sun, but a mother's work is never done.

Anonymous

...her candle goeth not out by night.

Proverbs 31:18

Worry is like a rocking chair: It gives you something to do, but doesn't get you anywhere.

Anonymous

Casting the whole of your care – all your anxieties, all your worries, all your concerns, once and for all – on Him; for He cares for you affectionately, and cares about you watchfully.

1 Peter 5:7 AMP

*I*f you have no prayer
life yourself, it is rather
a useless gesture to
make your child say
his prayers every night.

Peter Marshall

Pray without ceasing.
1 Thessalonians 5:17

The darn trouble with cleaning the house is it gets dirty the next day anyway, so skip a week if you have to. The children are the most important thing.

Barbara Bush

Lo, children are an heritage of the Lord: and the fruit of the womb is his reward.

Psalm 127:3

*I*f there is anything we wish
to change in the child,
we should first examine it
and see whether it is not
something that could be
better changed in ourselves.

C.G. Jung

*First take the beam out of your own eye, and then you will see
clearly to take out the speck that is in your brother's eye.*

Luke 6:42c AMP

I remember my mother's prayers and they have always followed me. They have clung to me all my life.

Abraham Lincoln

I prayed for this child, and the Lord has granted me what I asked of him.

1 Samuel 1:27 NIV

A problem not worth praying about isn't worth worrying about.

Glen Wheeler

—▸·◂—

Be careful for nothing; but in every thing
by prayer and supplication with thanksgiving
let your requests be made known unto God.

Philippians 4:6

Any child will learn to worship God who lives his daily life with adults who worship Him.

Anna B. Mow

He who walks with the wise grows wise....
Proverbs 13:20 NIV

*L*ook around you and
be distressed,
Look within you and
be depressed,
Look to Jesus and be at rest.

Anonymous

Looking unto Jesus the author and finisher of our faith....
Hebrews 12:2

A mother's love is patient and forgiving when all others are forsaking, and it never fails or falters, even though the heart is breaking.

Helen Steiner Rice

Love is patient, love is kind. It does not envy, it does not boast, it is not proud. Love never fails.

1 Corinthians 13:4,8a NIV

*M*aking children a part of a family team is of critical importance to the kinds of adults that they will become.

Dr. William Mitchell and Dr. Charles Paul Conn

Behold, how good and how pleasant it is for brethren to dwell together in unity!

Psalm 133:1

There is no greater
love than the love
that holds on where
there seems nothing
left to hold on to.

G.W.C. Thomas

*Love never fails – never fades out or
becomes obsolete or comes to an end.*

1 Corinthians 13:8a AMP

*E*very mother is like Moses. She does not enter the promised land. She prepares a world she will not see.

Pope Paul VI

Then the Lord said to him, "This is the land I promised on oath to Abraham, Isaac and Jacob.... I have let you see it with your eyes, but you will not cross over into it."

Deuteronomy 34:4 NIV

God sends children for another purpose than merely to keep up the race — to enlarge our hearts, to make us unselfish, and full of kindly sympathies and affections....

Mary Howitt

My little children, let us not love in word, neither in tongue; but in deed and in truth.

1 John 3:18

*E*very mother has the breathtaking privilege of sharing with God in the creation of new life. She helps bring into existence a soul that will endure for all eternity.

James Keller

For Thou didst form my inward parts;
Thou didst weave me in my mother's womb.

Psalm 139:13 NAS

We need to be patient
with our children in
the same way God
is patient with us.

Renee Jordan

The discretion of a man deferreth his anger;
and it is his glory to pass over a transgression.
Proverbs 19:11

A child is a gift whose worth cannot be measured except by the heart.

Theresa Ann Hunt

Behold, children are a gift of the Lord;
The fruit of the womb is a reward.

Psalm 127:3 NAS

*M*y mother said to me, "If you become a soldier you'll be a general; if you become a monk you'll end up as the pope." Instead, I became a painter and wound up as Picasso.

Pablo Picasso

(Love)...believeth all things, hopeth all things, endureth all things.

1 Corinthians 13:7

Our children are watching us live, and what we *are* shouts louder than anything we can *say*.

Wilferd A. Peterson

In everything set them an example by doing what is good.

Titus 2:7a NIV

*H*appy is the child . . .
who sees mother and
father rising early,
or going aside regularly,
to keep times with the Lord.

Larry Christenson

*...let the heart of them rejoice that seek the Lord. Seek the Lord,
and his strength: seek his face evermore.*

Psalm 105:3,4

You can do everything
else right as a parent,
but if you don't
begin with loving God,
you're going to fail.

Alvin Vander Griend

*...The Lord our God is one Lord: and thou shalt
love the Lord thy God with all thine heart,
and with all thy soul, and with all thy might.*

Deuteronomy 6:4,5

*B*eautiful as seemed Mama's face, it became incomparably more lovely when she smiled, and seemed to enliven everything about her.

Leo Tolstoy

...for the joy of the Lord is your strength.
Nehemiah 8:10

Daily prayers will diminish your cares.

Betty Mills

*Evening, and morning, and at noon, will I pray,
and cry aloud: and he shall hear my voice.*

Psalm 55:17

*M*ercy among the virtues is like the moon among the stars...It is the light that hovers above the judgement seat.

Edwin Hubbel Chapin

...mercy triumphs over judgment.

James 2:13 NAS

Nothing has a better effect upon children than praise.

Sir P. Sidney

*Anxiety in the heart of a man weighs it down,
But a good word makes it glad.*

Proverbs 12:25 NAS

A house without love
may be a castle, or a
palace, but it is not a
home; love is the life
of a true home.

John Lubbock

*Better a dry crust with peace and quiet
than a house full of feasting, with strife.*

Proverbs 17:1 NIV

*M*any a man has kept straight because his mother bent her knees.

Glen Wheeler

*. . . The earnest prayer of a righteous man
has great power and wonderful results.*

James 5:16 TLB

The more a child
becomes aware of a
mother's willingness to
listen, the more a mother
will begin to hear.

*A wise man will hear, and will increase learning;
and a man of understanding shall attain unto wise counsels.*

Proverbs 1:5

I remember leaving the hospital...thinking, "Wait, are they going to let me just walk off with him? I don't know beans about babies!"

Anne Tyler

If any of you lack wisdom, let him ask of God, that giveth to all men liberally, and upbraideth not; and it shall be given him.

James 1:5

A sweater is a garment worn by a child when his mother feels chilly.

Barbara Johnson

She has no fear of winter for her household, for she has made warm clothes for all of them.

Proverbs 31:21 TLB

*F*ingerprinting children is a good idea. It will settle the question as to who used the guest towel in the bathroom.

Unknown

But test everything that is said to be sure it is true, and if it is, then accept it.

1 Thessalonians 5:21 TLB

*A*ny mother could perform the jobs of several air-traffic controllers with ease.

Lisa Alther

She looketh well to the ways of her household, and eateth not the bread of idleness.

Proverbs 31:27

Parents must get across the idea that, "I love you always, but sometimes I do not love your behavior."

Amy Vanderbilt

Those whom I love, I reprove and discipline;
be zealous therefore, and repent.

Revelation 3:19 NAS

Level with your child by being honest. Nobody spots a phony quicker than a child.

M. MacCracken

...in all things willing to live honestly.

Hebrews 13:18

*A*s parents, we never stand so tall as when we stoop to help our children.

Dr. Anthony P. Witham

Be humble, thinking of others as better than yourself. Don't just think about your own affairs, but be interested in others, too, and in what they are doing. Your attitude should be the kind that was shown us by Jesus Christ.

Philippians 2:3b-5 TLB

A good laugh is sunshine in a house.

Thackeray

The light in the eyes (of him whose heart is joyful) rejoices the hearts of others....

Proverbs 15:30 AMP

$\mathcal{E}$ach loving act says
loud and clear,
"I love you. God loves
you. I care. God cares."

Joyce Heinrich and Annette LaPlaca

*Beloved, let us love one another: for love is of God;
and every one that loveth is born of God. . .for God is love.*

1 John 4:7,8

Children have more need of models than of critics.

Joseph Joubert

. . . Be their ideal; let them follow the way you teach and live; be a pattern for them in your love, your faith, and your clean thoughts.

1 Timothy 4:12 TLB

*I*t is better to keep children to their duty by a sense of honor and by kindness than by fear.

Terence

...do not irritate and provoke your children to anger – do not exasperate them to resentment – but rear them (tenderly) in the training and discipline and the counsel and admonition of the Lord.

Ephesians 6:4 AMP

(Encouragement) is the art of "turning your children on," helping them to do for themselves, not doing for them.

Dr. William Mitchell and Dr. Charles Paul Conn

*And thou shalt teach them ordinances and laws,
and shalt show them the way wherein they
must walk, and the work that they must do.*

Exodus 18:20

Home, sweet home — where each lives for the other, and all live for God.

T.J. Bach

For none of us lives to himself alone and none of us dies to himself alone. If we live, we live to the Lord; and if we die, we die to the Lord. So, whether we live or die, we belong to the Lord.

Romans 14:7,8 NIV

*C*hildren have never been very good at listening to their elders, but they have never failed to imitate them.

James Baldwin

...as ye know what manner of men we were among you for your sake. And ye became followers of us....

1 Thessalonians 1:5,6

$\mathcal{A}$ baby is God's opinion that the world should go on.

Carl Sandburg

And God blessed them, and God said unto them, Be fruitful, and multiply, and replenish the earth, and subdue it....

Genesis 1:28

A mother...fills a place so great that there isn't an angel in heaven who wouldn't be glad to give a bushel of diamonds to come down here and take her place.

Billy Sunday

And the angel came in unto her, and said, Hail, thou that art highly favoured, the Lord is with thee: blessed art thou among women.

Luke 1:28

I have held many things
in my hands and lost
them all; but the things
I have placed in God's hands,
those I always possess.

Earline Steelburg

*...for I know whom I have believed, and am
persuaded that he is able to keep that which
I have committed unto him against that day.*

2 Timothy 1:12

A mother is the one who is still there when everyone else has deserted you.

Anonymous

*If you love someone you will be loyal
to him no matter what the cost.*

1 Corinthians 13:7 TLB

A good deed is never lost; he who sows courtesy reaps friendship, and he who plants kindness gathers love.

St. Basil

———•———

. . .for whatsoever a man soweth, that shall he also reap. And let us not be weary in well doing: for in due season we shall reap, if we faint not.

Galatians 6:7,9

$\mathcal{E}$very word and deed of
a parent is a fiber woven
into the character of a child
that ultimately determines
how that child fits into the
fabric of society.

David Wilkerson

*You will be judged on whether or not you are doing what
Christ wants you to. So watch what you do and what you think.*

James 2:12 TLB

When people ask me what I do, I always say I am a mother first.

Jacqueline Jackson

Many women do noble things, but you surpass them all.
Proverbs 31:29 NIV

I think that saving a little child
And bringing him to his own,
Is a derned sight better
business
Than loafing around the throne.

John Hay

*The fruit of the righteous is a tree of life;
and he that winneth souls is wise.*

Proverbs 11:30

A mother's patience is like a tube of toothpaste — it's never quite gone.

Unknown

Being strengthened with all power according to his glorious might so that you may have great endurance and patience.

Colossians 1:11

The school will teach children how to read, but the environment of the home must teach them what to read. The school can teach them how to think, but the home must teach them what to believe.

Charles A. Wells

*Teach a child to choose the right path,
and when he is older he will remain upon it.*

Proverbs 22:6 TLB

Think of the sacrifice your mother had to make in order that you might live. Think of the sacrifice God had to make that you and your mother might live.

Glen Wheeler

This is love: not that we loved God, but that he loved us and sent his Son as an atoning sacrifice for our sins.

1 John 4:10 NIV

$\mathcal{K}$ind words can be short and easy to speak, but their echoes are truly endless.

Mother Teresa

She opens her mouth in skillful and godly Wisdom,
and on her tongue is the law of kindness
(giving counsel and instruction).

Proverbs 31:26 AMP

God has given you your child, that the sight of him, from time to time, might remind you of His goodness, and induce you to praise Him with filial reverence.

Christian Scriver

See how very much our heavenly Father loves us, for he allows us to be called his children — think of it — and we really are!

1 John 3:1 TLB

Your children learn more of your faith during the bad times than they do during the good times.

Beverly LaHaye

Consider it all joy, my brethren,
when you encounter various trials.

James 1:2 NAS

A woman who can cope with the terrible twos can cope with anything.

Judity Clabes

The Lord is on my side; I will not fear: what can man do unto me?

Psalm 118:6

*P*arenthood is a partnership
with God. . . .you are
working with the Creator
of the universe in shaping
human character and
determining destiny.

Ruth Vaughn

We are labourers together with God. . . .
1 Corinthians 3:9

Who ran to me when I fell,
And would some pretty
story tell,
Or kiss the place to
make it well?
My mother.

Ann Taylor

As one whom his mother comforted, so will I comfort you. . . .
Isaiah 66:13

Remember, when your child has a tantrum, don't have one of your own.

Dr. J. Kuriansky

And every man that striveth for the mastery is temperate in all things.

1 Corinthians 9:25a

The only thing children
wear out faster
than shoes are
parents and teachers.

He gives power to the tired and worn out,
and strength to the weak.

Isaiah 40:29 TLB

A little boy, age eight, gave a profound definition of parenthood: "Parents are just baby-sitters for God."

Glen Wheeler

I prayed for this child, and the Lord has granted me what I asked of him. So now I give him to the Lord. For his whole life he will be given over to the Lord....

1 Samuel 1:27,28 NIV

*M*y mother was the source from which I derived the guiding principles of my life.

John Wesley

Be ye followers of me, even as I also am of Christ.

1 Corinthians 11:1

HUMOROUS QUOTES SECTION

A merry heart doeth
good like a medicine....
Proverbs 17:22

There is a right time for
everything: A time to laugh....
Ecclesiastes 3:1,4 TLB

Never lend your car to anyone to whom you have given birth.

Erma Bombeck

A merry heart doeth good like a medicine....
Proverbs 17:22

Parenthood: that state of being better chaperoned than you were before marriage.

Madeline Cox

There is a right time for everything: A time to laugh....
Ecclesiastes 3:1,4 TLB

The best way to keep children at home is to make home a pleasant atmosphere — and to let the air out of the tires.

Dorothy Parker

A merry heart doeth good like a medicine....
Proverbs 17:22

A mother finds
out what is meant
by spitting image
when she tries to feed
cereal to her baby.

Imogene Fey

There is a right time for everything: A time to laugh....
Ecclesiastes 3:1,4 TLB

A lot of parents pack up their troubles and send them off to summer camp.

Raymond Duncan

A merry heart doeth good like a medicine....
Proverbs 17:22

*A*dult education is something that will continue as long as kids have homework.

Unknown

There is a right time for everything: A time to laugh....

Ecclesiastes 3:1,4 TLB

Small boy: "If I'm noisy they give me a spanking...and if I'm quiet they take my temperature."

Coronet

A merry heart doeth good like a medicine....

Proverbs 17:22

*P*arents of teens and parents
of babies have something
in common. They spend
a great deal of time trying
to get their kids to talk.

Paul Swets

There is a right time for everything: A time to laugh....
Ecclesiastes 3:1,4 TLB

People who say they sleep like a baby usually don't have one.

Leo J. Burke

A merry heart doeth good like a medicine....
Proverbs 17:22

A perfect example
of minority rule is a
baby in the house.

Milwaukee Journal

There is a right time for everything: A time to laugh....
Ecclesiastes 3:1,4 TLB

*I*f evolution really works, how come mothers have only two hands?

Ed Dussault

A merry heart doeth good like a medicine....
Proverbs 17:22

*T*he best time to give
children your advise is
when they are young
enough to believe you know
what you are talking about.

Unknown

➤━━ · ━━◄

There is a right time for everything: A time to laugh....
Ecclesiastes 3:1,4 TLB

*A*sk your child what he wants for dinner only if he's buying.

Fran Lebowitz

A merry heart doeth good like a medicine....
Proverbs 17:22

Children are a great comfort in your old age — and they help you reach it faster, too.

Lionel M. Kaufman

There is a right time for everything: A time to laugh....
Ecclesiastes 3:1,4 TLB

The quickest way for a parent to get a child's attention is to sit down and look comfortable.

Lane Olinhouse

A merry heart doeth good like a medicine....
Proverbs 17:22

Children certainly brighten up a home. Did you ever see a child under 12 turn off an electric light?

Unknown

There is a right time for everything: A time to laugh....
Ecclesiastes 3:1,4 TLB

*M*an has his will —
but woman has her way.

Oliver Wendell Holmes

A merry heart doeth good like a medicine....
Proverbs 17:22

A food is not necessarily essential just because your child hates it.

Katherine Whitehouse

There is a right time for everything: A time to laugh....
Ecclesiastes 3:1,4 TLB

Cleaning your house while your kids are still growing is like shoveling the walk before it stops snowing.

Phyllis Diller

A merry heart doeth good like a medicine....
Proverbs 17:22

Children often hold a marriage together — by keeping their parents too busy to quarrel with each other.

The Saturday Evening Post

There is a right time for everything: A time to laugh....
Ecclesiastes 3:1,4 TLB

A baby is an angel whose wings decrease as his legs increase.

French Proverb

A merry heart doeth good like a medicine....
Proverbs 17:22

A suburban mother's role is to deliver children obstetrically once, and by car forever after.

Peter DeVries

There is a right time for everything: A time to laugh....
Ecclesiastes 3:1,4 TLB

*A*ny time a child can be seen but not heard, it's a shame to wake him.

Unknown

A merry heart doeth good like a medicine....
Proverbs 17:22

*I*nsomnia: a contagious disease often transmitted from babies to parents.

Shannon Fife

There is a right time for everything: A time to laugh....
Ecclesiastes 3:1,4 TLB

*F*amiliarity breeds contempt — and children.

Mark Twain

A merry heart doeth good like a medicine....
Proverbs 17:22